Rhythm Book 102 Eighth Note Rhythm Patterns

Taura Eruera

Rhythm Book 102 Eighth Note Rhythm Patterns

Published by Hookmedia Co Ltd

Hookmedia Co Ltd

© Copyright Taura Eruera 2006. All Rights Reserved.

Email: hookmediapublications@gmail.com

National Library of New Zealand

ISBN 0-9582254-5-1
Kindle ISBN 0-9582254-6-X

Rhythm Book Series

Rhythm Book 101	Quarter Note Rhythm Patterns. The *Dobodobo* Rhythms
Rhythm Book 102	Eighth Note Rhythm Patterns. The *Dabadaba* Rhythms
Rhythm Book 103	Sixteenth Note Rhythm Patterns. The *Dibidibi* Rhythms
Rhythm Book 104	Triplet Eighth Note Rhythm Patterns. The *Pataka Pataka* Rhythms
Rhythm Book 105	Triplet Eighth Note Rhythm Patterns. The Syncopated *Pataka Pataka* Rhythms
Rhythm Book 106	Quarter Note Rhythm Patterns. The *Dobobo* Rhythms
Rhythm Book 107	Eighth Note Rhythm Patterns. The *Dababa* Rhythms
Rhythm Book 201	Quarter Note Rhythm Patterns. The *Dobodobo Dobodobo* Rhythms
Rhythm Book 202	Eighth Note Rhythm Patterns. The *Dabadaba Dabadaba* Rhythms
Rhythm Book 203	Sixteenth Note Rhythm Patterns. The *Dibidibi Dibidibi* Rhythms

For Chiefy Pakinga, my first music teacher, who taught me ukulele informally at 9 years old and entertained the whole Cadness Street neighborhood with his amazing steel and slide guitar playing on his front porch, in those halcyon days before color television.

"I would often learn to say the rhythm before I learned to beat it, and [*my teacher*] would correct my mistakes by speaking the proper rhythm."

African Rhythm and African Sensibility, John Miller Chernoff (78:1981)

Reader's Note

If you have read Rhythm Book 101 Quarter Note Rhythm Patterns

You can fast track this book: read the Dabadaba Vocabulary on pages 4-5; then read the Learn Sixteen Dabadaba Sounds with Notation Instructions on pages V-XV in the appendices (9 minutes); then go straight into talking the 758 bars of Dabadaba rhythm from pages 9-102 (25 minutes without breaks, 40 minutes with energy breaks, 60 minutes with text and energy breaks); then read the Introduction, Chapter Texts, FAQS and Glossary entries as you need them.

If you have not read Rhythm Book 101 Quarter Note Rhythm Patterns

I recommend you take ninety-nine minutes to read the Rhythm Book 101 before reading this book.

Contents

Introduction 1
   Chapter One: Talk 8 Attack Rhythm 9
   Chapter Two: Talk 7 Attack Rhythms 11
   Chapter Three: Talk 6 Attack Rhythms 15
   Chapter Four: Talk 5 Attack Rhythms 25
   Chapter Five: Talk 4 Attack Rhythms 39
   Chapter Six: Talk 3 Attack Rhythms 61
   Chapter Seven: Talk 2 Attack Rhythms 75
   Chapter Eight: Talk 1 Attack Rhythms 87
   Chapter Nine: Talk Syncopated Rhythms 91
   Chapter Ten: What You Have Learned 103

How To Learn Dabadaba Words I
   Learn Sixteen Dabadaba Words in 8 Bar Sections I
   Learn Sixteen Dabadaba Sounds with Notation Instructions V
   Learn Sixteen Dabadaba Words in 12 Bar Sections XVI
   Learn Sixteen Dabadaba Words in 16 Bar Sections XVI
   Learn Sixteen Dabadaba Words in 32 Bar Sections XVI

Frequently Asked Questions XVII
   Why does saying the d and b in the prescribed place matter? XVII
   How does saying the d and b in the prescribed place help a rhythm guitar player? XVII
   How is each rhythm derived from dabadaba? XVII
   Do I keep the tempo in my hands or feet? XIX
   Do you count rhythm with rhythmisation? XXI
   Is Rhythmisation the only rhythm verbalisation system? XXI
   How does knowing dobodobo help the jazz, rock and pop musician? XXII
   How does knowing dobodobo help the blues and reggae musician? XXII
   How does dobodobo help with odd subdivisions? XXII
   What is the principle of rhythmic alternation? XXIII
   What's an example of a dabadaba song? XXIV

Rhythmisation Glossary XXV

About the Author XXXIII
   Join Rhythmisation Insights XXXV

Introduction

Welcome to Rhythm Book 102 Eighth Note Rhythm Patterns for All Musicians.

In the next forty-nine minutes, or so, you could feasibly read every word--and *talk* every rhythm--in this book. In less than nine minutes you can learn a dabadaba vocabulary of sixteen, eighth note, rhythms from scratch. Then, in the remaining time, using this vocabulary, you can--to your possible surprise and absolute delight--talk seven hundred and fifty-eight bars of dabadaba rhythms.

This book is a *doing* book. It is not a thinking book. I do not attempt to explain an experience you have not yet had. I give you an experience first, then, invite you to reflect on what you learned from that.

To that end, my introductory comments will be as brief as possible. As I write I am keeping in mind the question: what is the *least* you need to know to successfully complete this book?

The first point to note is that this whole book is based on only *one rhythm*: the eighth note rhythm. This entire book is about talking eighth note rhythms *derived* from this one rhythm.

In this book we refer to this seed rhythm as the dabadaba rhythm. This parent rhythm is displayed here.

In this bar you see five horizontal lines, called a stave, a G treble clef, a 2/4 time signature and four eighth notes or four quavers. All these aspects are lumped under the heading of music notation.

Under the first and third eighth notes is the syllable da. Under the second and fourth eighth notes is the syllable ba. The vowel, a, in da and ba is pronounced the same as the vowel, a, in path. Any syllable displaying under a note is called a rhythmisation syllable.

These syllables form the word dabadaba. Dabadaba is the rhythmisation for a bar of four eighth notes.

In the seven hundred and fifty-eight bars that follow I ask you to take no notice of the stave, clef and time signature but focus only on the rhythm notes and rhythmisation.

Rhythmisation is to rhythm what solmisation (solfa or solfeggio) is to melodic pitch. Just as do re mi uniquely describes the sound of the first three notes of a major scale so does dabadaba *uniquely* describe a bar, or group, of four eighth notes.

Rhythmisation is a system for verbalising rhythm. Rhythmisation is the language we use to talk the dabadaba vocabulary in this book.

The dabadaba *vocabulary* consists of several rhythms *derived* from this seed rhythm.

We concern ourselves with only sixteen of them in this book.

When we talk about dabadaba we are talking about a rhythm *level*. When we talk about the dabadaba's, we are talking about the dabadaba rhythm *vocabulary*. When we talk about a dabadaba rhythm we are talking about any rhythm that is a *member* of this vocabulary.

Talking the sixteen rhythms is simple. **The dabadaba vocabulary uses three vowels** pronounced as follows: a as in bath, o as in go, u as in blue.

As you can see, vowel pronunciation is simple. Pronouncing vowel *duration* or vowel length is not so simple for native English speakers because vowel length is not significant in English conversation.

For example, if you say the word movie, with a really long o sound or short one, the meaning remains the same. The upshot is that learning to talk five different durations--for five different vowels--is a new experience, for most monolingual English speakers.

All vowels are all different lengths.

The **a** vowel is one half beat long.

The **o** vowel is one click or one beat long.

The **u** vowel is two clicks or two beats long.

The **ao** and **oa** diphthongs are one and a half beats long.

Please note that in this book, one metronome click measures one beat.

The consonants, **d**, **b** and **s** are pronounced as normal.

Attacks and Syllables

In any rhythmisation vocabulary, the rhythms are grouped by *attacks*. An attack signals where any rhythm duration starts. Durations may be sounded or not sounded. A *sounded* duration is indicated by any d or b consonant. An *unsounded* duration is indicated by an s consonant. An unsounded duration is called a rest.

The attack status of a rhythm does not count every syllable in a word. Only sounded syllables are counted. This is why s*a*badaba is counted as a three attack rhythm, s*o*daba as a two attack rhythm, s*a*bao as a one attack rhythm and s*u* as a nil attack rhythm.

The rhythms in the dabadaba vocabulary are presented in groups of 4 attacks, 3 attacks, 2 attacks, 1 attack and 0 attack rhythms.

Dabadaba Vocabulary in Notation and Rhythmisation

Here is the dabadaba vocabulary presented in notation and rhythmisation, grouped by attacks.

Dabadaba Vocabulary

Rhythmisation by Taura Eruera

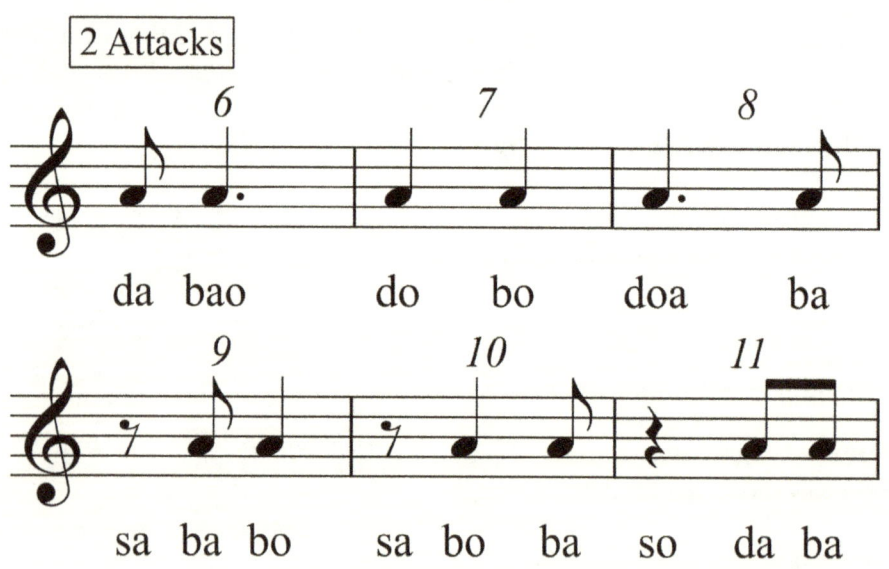

Dabadaba Vocabulary in Rhythmisation

Here is the sixteen word vocabulary, presented in rhythmisation only.

4 attacks: dabadaba.

3 attacks: dababo, daboba, dodaba, sabadaba.

2 attacks: dabao, dobo, doaba, sababo, saboba, sodaba.

1 attack: du, sabao, sobo, soaba.

0 attack: su.

Syncopated rhythms: daboba, dabao, doaba, dababo, dabao.

How Do You Learn The Rhythm Words?

Because of the vowel duration challenges mentioned earlier, it is important that you take time to *actually* learn to pronounce each word in the vocabulary. By that, I mean, it's important that your brain *actually* encodes and archives the pronunciation of each word *accurately*, that your brain can retrieve each rhythm word on demand, that your speech system can *accurately* say each word on demand.

To build this skill, I recommend you turn your metronome on to MM60 and say each word 8 times. If you are saying each dabadaba word for the very first time, focus on relaxing all your speech muscles: lips, tongue and jaw as you accurately articulate each consonant, each vowel duration, each syllable and each rhythm word as a whole.

Notice how it feels to say each dabadaba word once, twice, four and eight times. Saying each word once *is* saying a one bar phrase. Saying it twice *is* saying a two bar, call and response phrase. Saying it four times *is* saying two, two bar, call and response phrases.

Saying any rhythm word eight times is effectively saying four, two bar, call and response phrases, or two, four bar, call and response phrases.

Notice the difference between saying a word on an odd bar and an even bar, a strong bar and a weak bar.

To follow detailed, step by step, instructions, refer to the Learn Sixteen Dabadaba Words in 8 Bar Sections in the appendices after page 104. You can also learn the dabadaba sounds with notation on pages VI-XV of the appendices. At MM60 this process will take you just over eight minutes.

Assuming you have learned the vocabulary, you are now ready to talk the big lot of dabadaba's, all seven hundred and fifty-eight of them.

This is not as scary as it might sound. You have already spoken each word a minimum of eight times. Over the next twenty-six minutes you will talk each word in the dabadaba vocabulary, several times, in several different contexts.

You will talk dabadaba 32 times across the 758 bars.

You will talk 3 attack rhythms, one hundred and eighty-five times: namely, dababo 41 times, daboba 62 times, dodaba 41 times and sabadaba, 41 times.

You will talk 2 attack rhythms, three hundred and twenty-one times: specifically, dabao 65 times, dobo 44 times, doaba 64 times, sababo 38 times, saboba 66 times and sodaba, 44 times.

You will talk 1 attack rhythms, one hundred and eighty-five times: specifically, du 21 times, bu 20 times, sabao 62 times, sobo 41 times and soaba, 41 times. Finally you will talk su 35 times.

You now know a lot. You now know how to pronounce each dabadaba word. You know how many times you are going to say each word. You know that you will be talking seven hundred and fifty-eight bars of dabadaba. You know that you will talking three hundred and sixty-three two bar, call and response, dabadaba phrases.

You know it will take you twenty-six minutes to read seven hundred and fifty-eight bars with no break between chapters (or forty minutes with energy breaks, or sixty minutes with text and energy breaks).

You know it's time for you to now launch yourself. Good luck.

Go talk yourself some dabadaba.

Chapter One: Talk 8 Attack Rhythm

In this chapter you talk only one rhythm: dabadaba, the parent rhythm for this vocabulary. Dabadaba occurs on both the first and second bar, that is, on both the strong and weak bar.

Dabadaba is the seed rhythm that the other fifteen dabadaba rhythms derive from. This is the *fundamental* rhythm that you need to articulate clearly and cleanly. In the initial stages, you will do so carefully and deliberately, then---after many, many repetitions over time---automatically.

In this chapter you want to really feel each beat division clearly. Feel each da clearly. Feel each ba clearly. Feel how dobo divides into dabadaba. Feel it in your imagination, your speech and your body.

Feel the strong part of the beat clearly. Feel the weak part of the beat clearly. Feel the down of the beat clearly. Feel the up of the beat clearly.

Feel the down of the click clearly. Feel the unsounded middle of the click clearly. Feel where the upbeat is in between metronome clicks.

Feeling the da and ba of each beat clearly is fundamental to feeling every rhythm in the dabadaba vocabulary. This is the skill required to be able to feel diphthong rhythms like doaba, and syncopations like daboba.

Notice the principle of rhythm alternation operating here, at the level of the beat and the bar. Notice what you notice about these beat (daba) and bar (strong-weak) alternations as you talk dabadaba.

This 8 attack rhythm has a (4 + 4) rhythm profile. The (4 + 4) profile means that the two bar phrase is made up of a 4 attack rhythm in the strong bar and a 4 attack rhythm in the weak bar.

Notice what is different *within* you as you say this rhythm. How does the strong bar feel to you? How does the weak bar feel to you? Why is dabadaba dabadaba called an 8 attack rhythm?

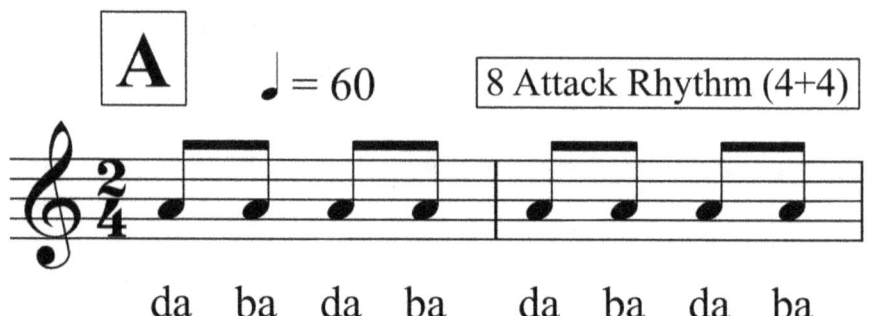

Chapter Two: Talk 7 Attack Rhythms

In this chapter you are talking 7 attack rhythms. That is, all the rhythms in this chapter display a *rhythm density* of 7 attacks. Rhythm density is a term that broadly describes how rhythmically active a rhythm phrase is.

You are talking only the first five words of the vocabulary--in different combinations—in this chapter. Clearly articulating the daba alternation you learned in chapter one helps you with talking your first syncopated rhythm in this book: the daboba rhythm.

In this chapter you are experiencing two bar, call and response phrases. The rhythm in the strong, odd numbered bar is the *calling rhythm* while the rhythm in the weak, even numbered bar, is the *responding rhythm*.

The rhythms in section B are called CV rhythms. The CV letters are initials, standing for *constant variable* rhythm which in turn, is shorthand, for a *constant rhythm* calling a *variable rhythm*. That is to say, in section B, a constant rhythm in a strong bar is answered by a variable rhythm in the weak bar.

In section C, the reverse occurs with VC phrasing. That is, a variable rhythm in the strong bar is answered by a constant rhythm in the weak bar.

In this chapter you are also being introduced to the concept of *rhythm profile*. In section B, the rhythm profile of these 7 attack rhythm phrases is (4 + 3). This means that there is a 4 attack rhythm being answered by a 3 attack rhythm.

In section C, the rhythm profile is (3 + 4): that is, a 3 attack rhythm on the strong bar is being answered by a 4 attack rhythm on the weak bar.

After you have talked these rhythm profiles, reflect on how (4 + 3) phrases felt the same and different to you, from (3 + 4) phrases? What did you notice?

C

7 Attack Rhythm (3+4) VC

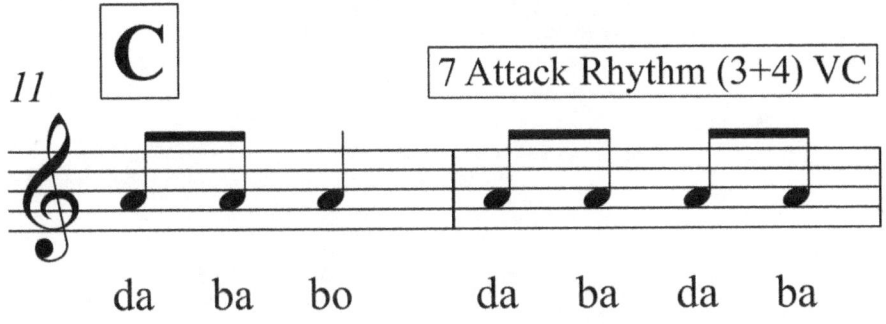

Chapter Three: Talk 6 Attack Rhythms

In this chapter you are talking 6 attack rhythms. That is, all the rhythms in this chapter display a *rhythm density* of 6 attacks.

For the first time, you will talk the 2 attack rhythms in this chapter: dabao, dobo, doaba, sababo, saboba, sodaba; in combination with the 4 attack dabadaba rhythm.

Combining 2 attack rhythms with a 4 attack rhythm will offer you *rhythm balance* insights that (3 + 3) rhythms do not.

In chapter two you met the three attack, daboba, syncopated rhythm. In this one you meet the two attack, saboba, syncopated rhythm.

For the first time in this talking section, you are meeting the two important, two attack, *diphthong rhythms*: dabao and doaba.

These rhythms are two attack derivations of three attack, rhythms: specifically, dabao from dababo, and doaba from dodaba (see appendices pages XVII-XIX for a detailed discussion of *derived rhythms*).

Repeatedly saying these rhythm pairs---dababo, dabao and dodaba, doaba---will guide you to the correct pronunciation for the dabao and doaba diphthongs.

You will also talk more 3 attack phrases, as both CV and VC phrases. You will get lots of practise talking 3 attack dabadaba rhythms. Again, you will reflect on how 3 attack CV phrases feel the same, or different, to you, as 3 attack VC phrases.

At the end of this chapter, take a moment to reflect on how, in your experience, (4 + 2) rhythms are similar or different to (2 + 4) rhythms. What do you notice?

How do the (3 + 3) phrases compare and contrast with the (2 + 4) and (4 + 2) phrases. What do you notice?

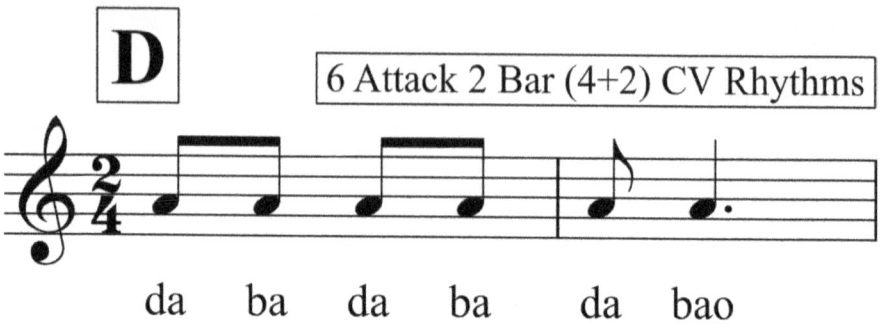

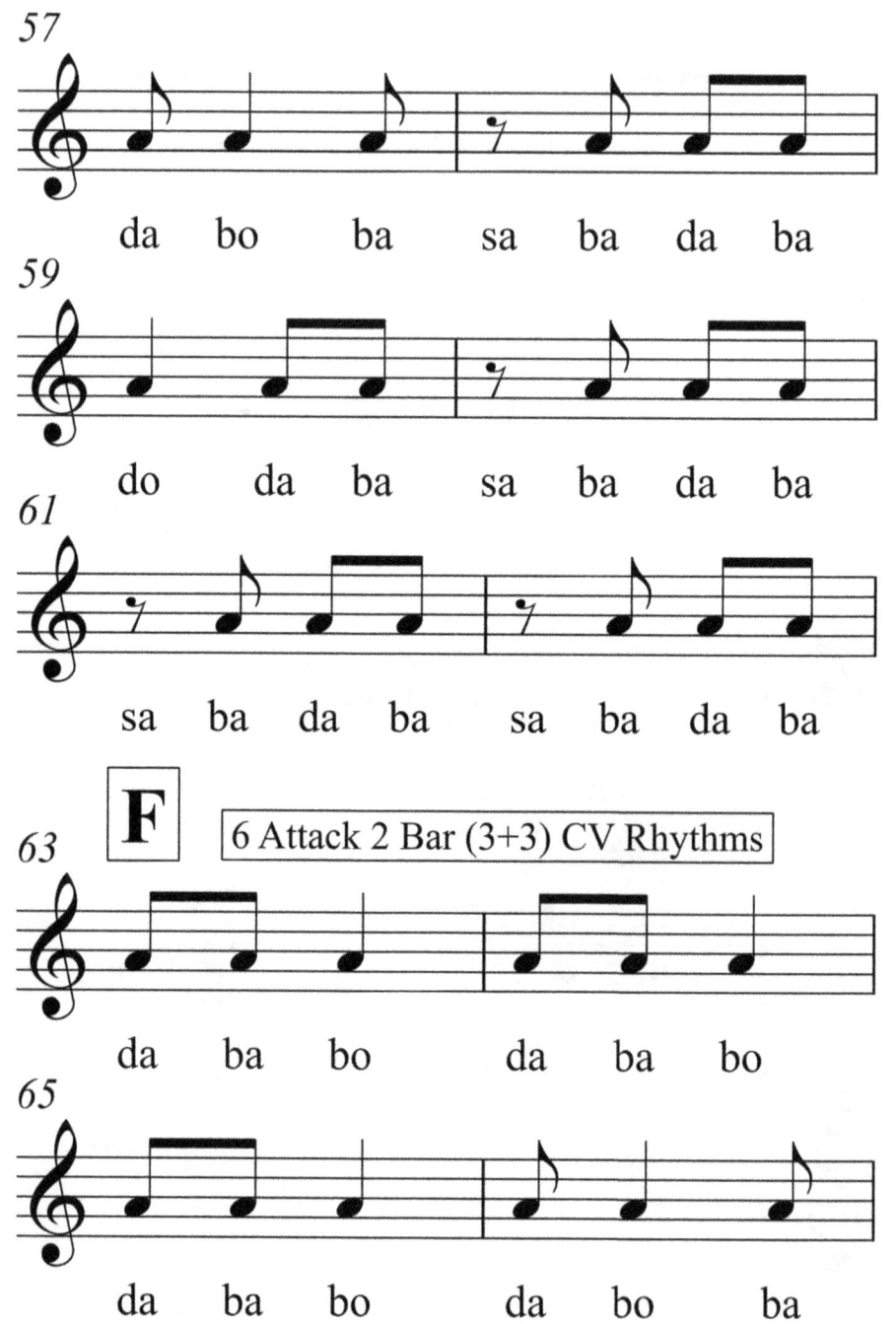

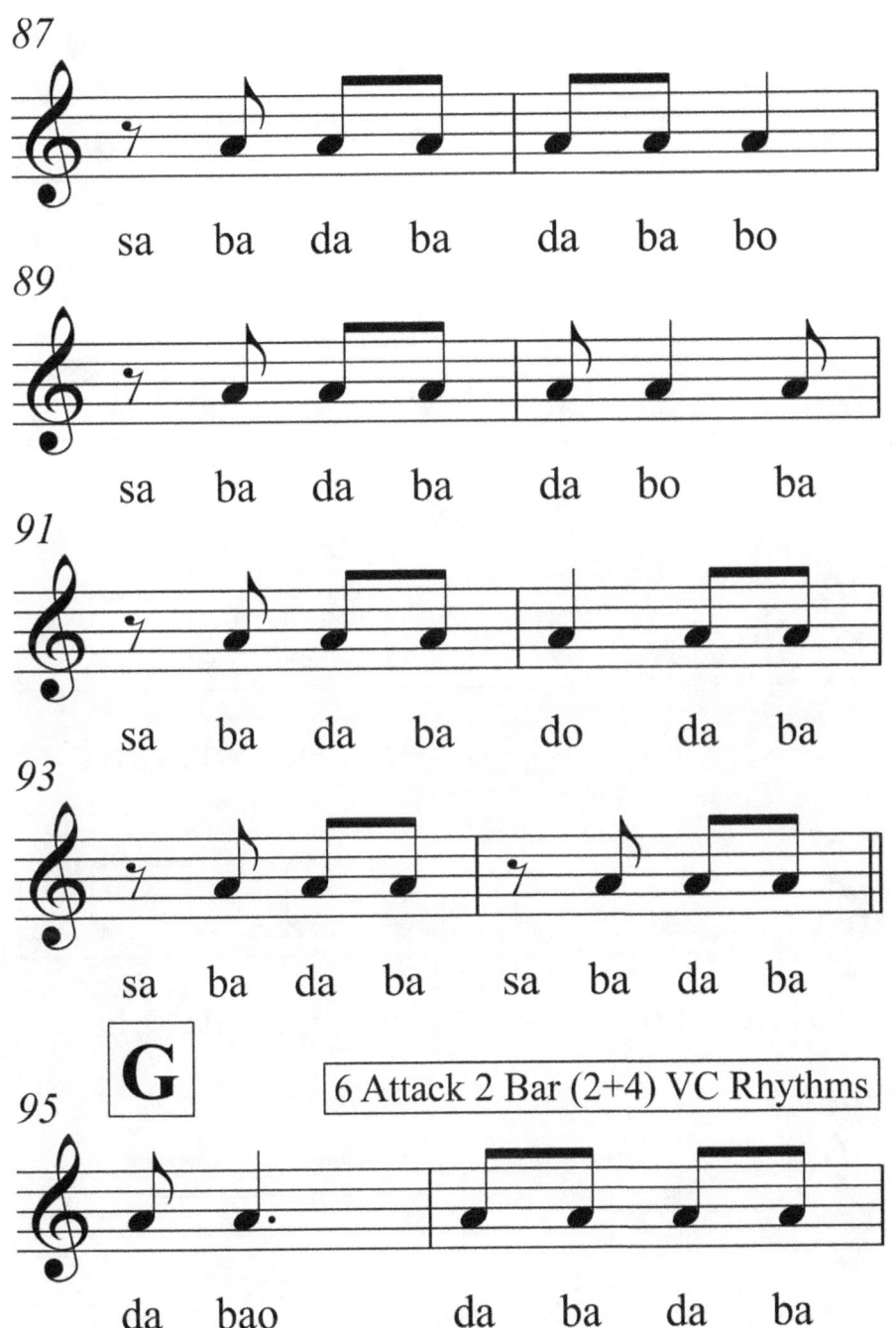

Chapter Four: Talk 5 Attack Rhythms

In this chapter you talk only dabadaba rhythms with a rhythm density of 5 attacks.

For the first time, you will talk the 1 attack rhythms in this chapter: du, sabao, sobo and soaba; in combination with the 4 attack dabadaba rhythm.

The two diphthong rhythms in this group are 1 attack derivations of 2 attack rhythms: specifically, sabao from dabao, and soaba from doaba. See appendices pages XVII-XIX for details about derived rhythms.

Saying these rhythm pairs repeatedly---dabao, sabao and doaba, soaba--- will guide you to the correct pronunciation for the sabao and soaba diphthong rhythms.

Rhythms like sabao, sobo and soaba illustrate an important rhythm guideline: *rests are as important as sounded notes.* This ability to articulate rests, is one of the unique features of rhythmisation generally, and of dabadaba, specifically.

This feature protects the beginner student from the common beginner trap: ignoring rests altogether and focusing only on sounded notes.

In section H you are talking (4 + 1) CV phrases. How does the balance of this dabadaba phrase feel to you when a 4 attack, strong bar, rhythm is answered by a 1 attack, weak bar rhythm?

Conversely, how does a (1 + 4) phrase in section K feel to you? What are the differences and similarities between a (1 + 4) and (4 + 1) dabadaba phrase? How do the differences and similarities feel to you?

Similarly, in your dabadaba experience, how do (3 + 2) VC rhythms in section I compare and contrast with (2 + 3) VC rhythms in section J?

In your view, how do (3 + 2) and (2 + 3) dabadaba rhythms compare, and contrast, with (1 + 4) and (4 + 1) quaver rhythms?

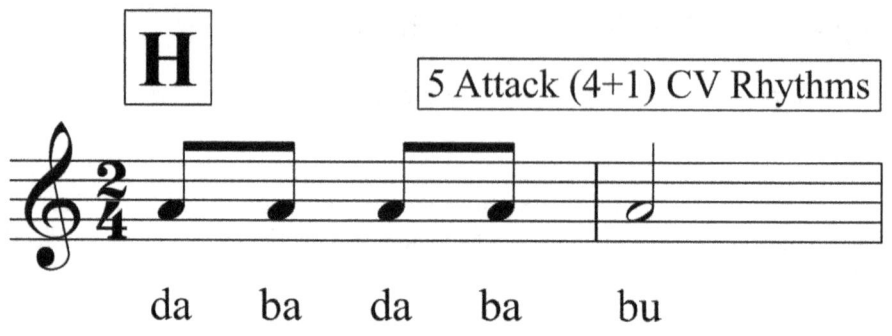

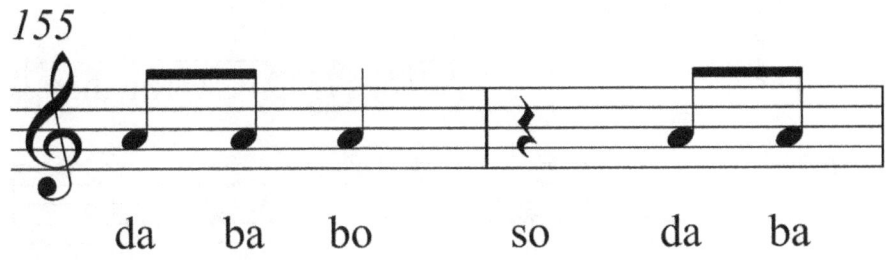

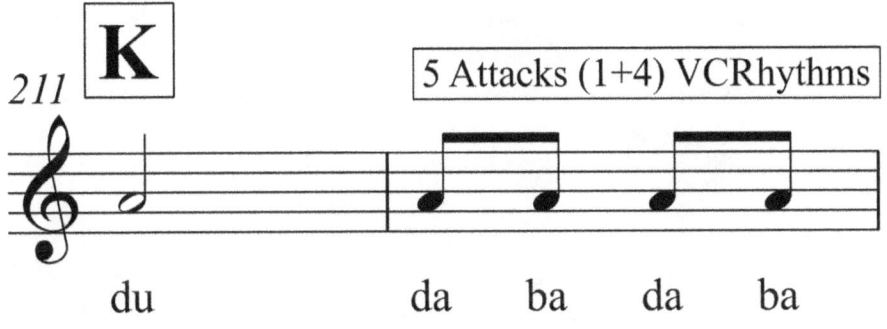

Chapter Five: Talk 4 Attack Rhythms

In this chapter you talk dabadaba rhythms with a rhythm density of 4 attacks.

For the first time, you talk the 0 attack rhythm, su, in this chapter: specifically, in the (4 + 0) and (0 +4) phrases. Again, take particular care in holding the u vowel for a full 2 clicks. Nothing less than the full value will work.

With the introduction of su in this chapter, you have now talked all the rhythms in the dabadaba vocabulary. Congratulations. You will meet no more new rhythms in the remainder of this book: just new combinations.

In this chapter you have one hundred, 4 attack, dabadaba phrases, at your disposal. That is, you have ninety-nine rhythm variations and substitutions available for any 4 attack rhythm. Through the following profiles, you have one hundred ways to say a 4 attack, dabadaba rhythm.

You have a (4 + 0) and a (0 + 4) phrase.

You have a selection of (3 + 1) CV and (1 + 3) VC phrases.

You have a selection of (2 + 2) VC and (2 + 2) CV phrases

Before you start talking these rhythms, think about what you expect the difference between a (4 + 0), and a (0 + 4), dabadaba rhythm, to feel like to you. Similarly, what differences would you expect to experience with (3 + 1) CV and (1 + 3) VC phrases? Again, what similarities and differences would you expect to experience with (2 + 2) VC and (2 + 2) CV phrases?

After you have talked this chapter, reflect on the same questions and see how your expectations lined up (or not) with your actual experience. This before-and-after process is not about finding any objectively right answer. It's about helping you think about rhythm and helping you *describe* how you think about rhythm.

A parting reminder: with the 1 attack and 2 attack rhythms, give great importance to articulating and saying the *rest* syllables in full.

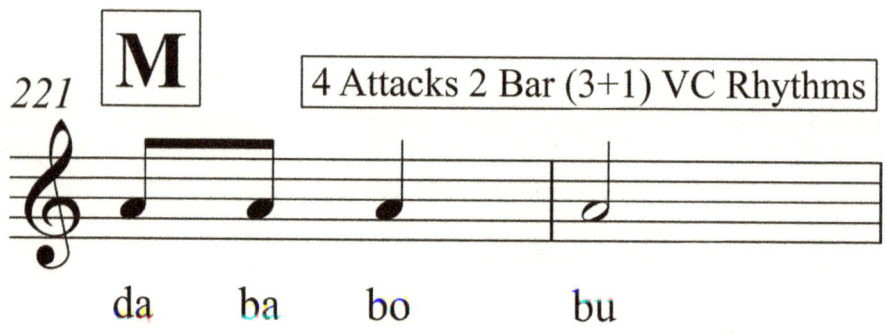

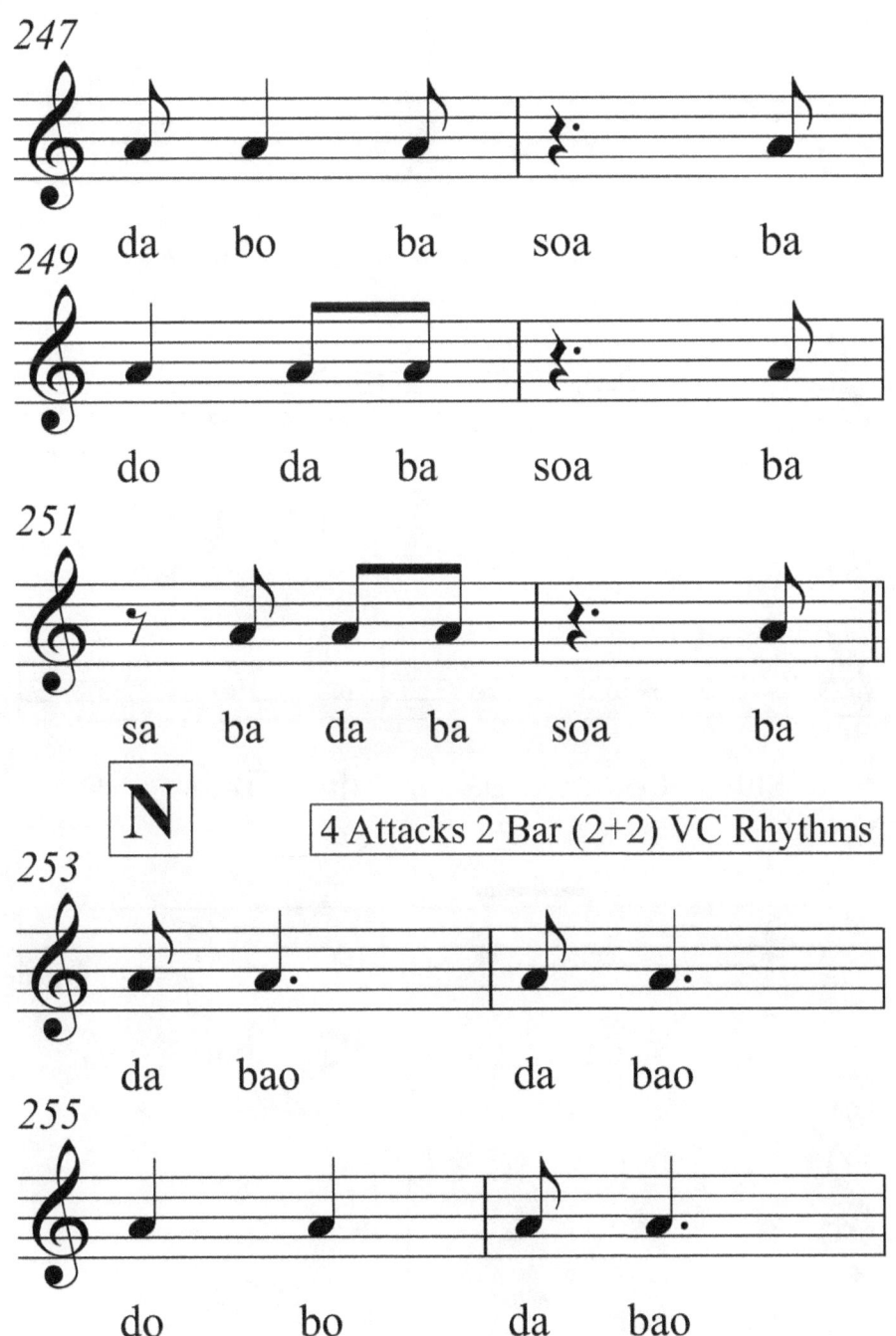

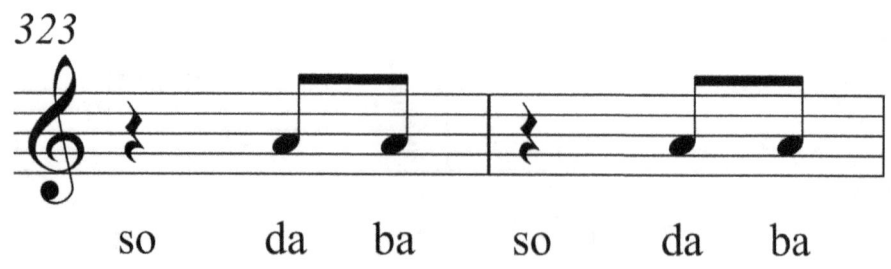

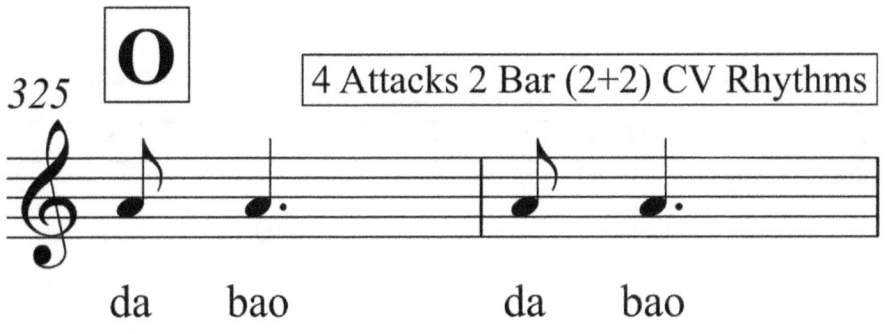

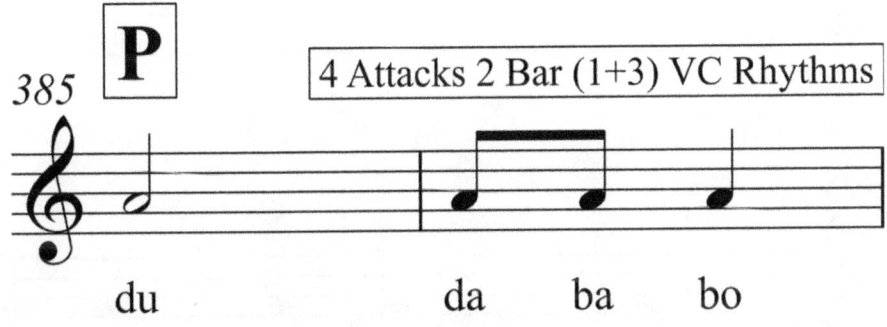

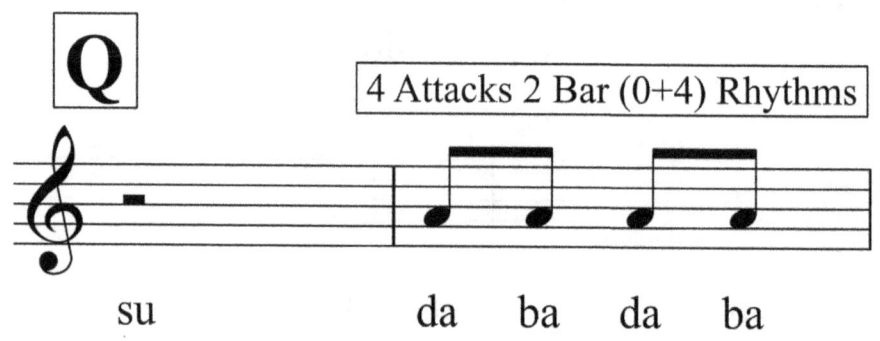

Chapter Six: Talk 3 Attack Rhythms

In this chapter you will talk two bar, dabadaba, phrases with a rhythm density of 3 attacks.

With 3 attack rhythms, only three notes are being attacked across four beats (and eight possible attacks). This means that five attacks are *not* being attacked and that these non-attacked spaces are being taken up with, either, long vowels, diphthongs or rests.

When you talk 3 attack rhythms you are, either, talking *attacked* long vowels or diphthongs--for their *full* duration—or, talking *rested* long vowels or diphthongs--for their *full* duration.

Generally speaking, the fewer the attacks employed, the more important the rests are. You must give primacy to *accurately* articulating the rests, the long vowels and diphthongs to make these rhythms work. Your pronunciation work in previous chapters will help you achieve this skill.

In this chapter you will talk (3 + 0) and (0 + 3) phrases. You will also talk (2 + 1) CV and (1 + 2) VC phrases. You will have 58 different ways to express a 3 attack, dabadaba, rhythm and fifty-seven *rhythm substitutes* for, and variations on, any 3 attack, quarter note, rhythm. That's worth remembering any time you have a 3 attack melody to improvise on, or compose variations for.

Before you start talking these dabadaba rhythms, think about what you expect the difference between a (3 + 0) and a (0 + 3) phrase to feel like. Similarly, what differences would you expect to experience with (2 + 1) CV and (1 + 2) VC phrases?

After you have talked this chapter, reflect on the same questions and see how your expectations lined up, or not, with your actual experience. Take note of your dabadaba insights and how they help you think about rhythm in and out of tempo.

The advice to nail the eighth note rhythms in this chapter is always worth repeating. Pay close attention to articulating rests and tied vowels in *full*.

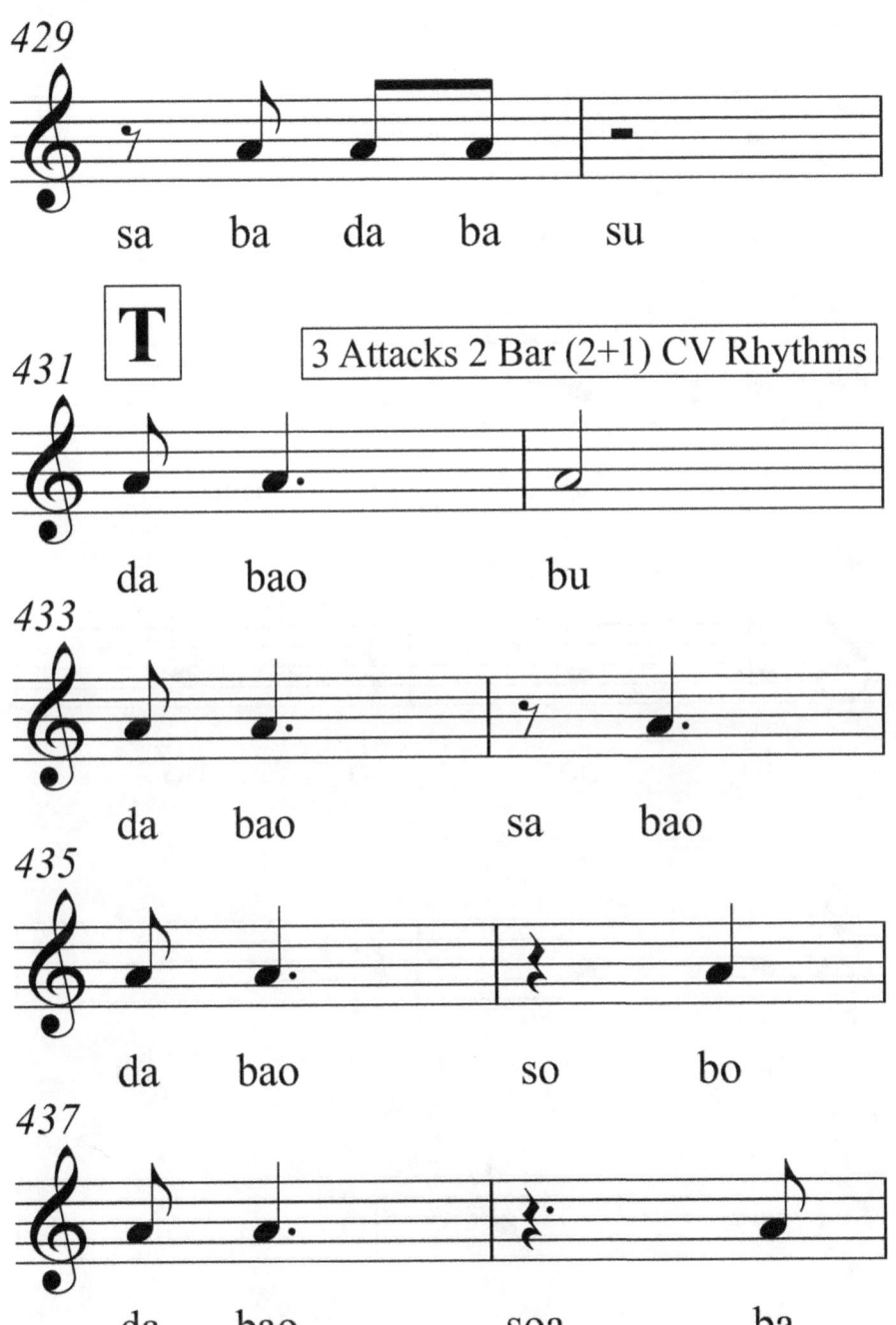

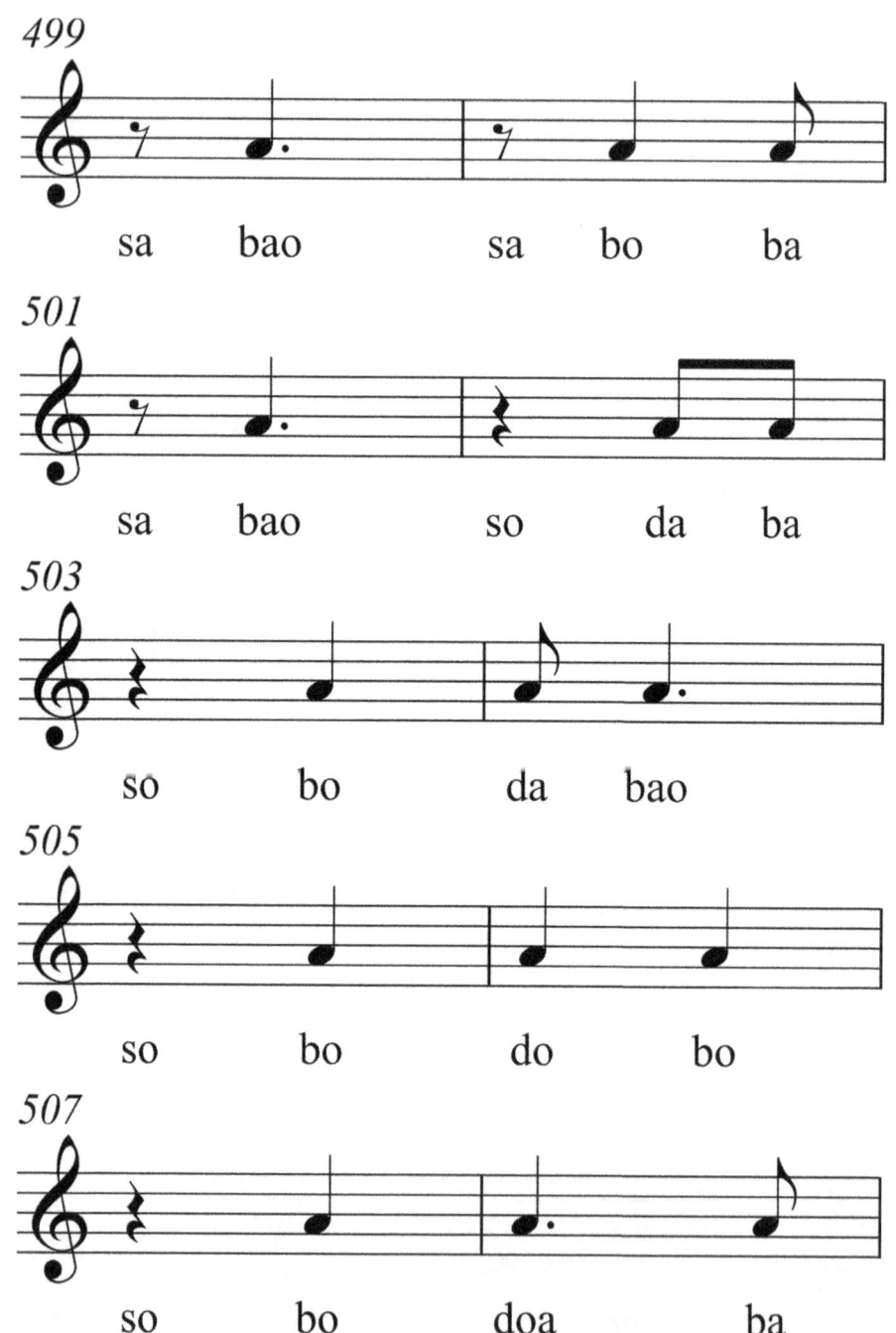

V

3 Attacks 2 Bar (0 + 3) Rhythms

527
su   da ba

529
su   da bo ba

531
su   do da ba

533
su   sa ba da ba

Chapter Seven: Talk 2 Attack Rhythms

In this chapter you talk dabadaba rhythms with a rhythm density of 2 attacks.

This means only two notes per two bar phrase are being attacked while six potential notes are not being attacked but are being occupied by long vowels, diphthongs or rests.

With 2 attack rhythms you are, either, talking attacked vowels or diphthongs--for their *full* duration—or, talking rested vowels or diphthongs--for their *full* duration.

With 2 attack rhythms, articulating rests and tied vowels or diphthongs accurately, are *critically* important to making these rhythms work. Fortunately, you met these dabadaba rhythms in chapter two. You have five chapters of experience, in articulating two attack rhythms, to bring to bear.

You met 1 attack rhythms in chapter four. You have two chapters of experience, in articulating 1 attack rhythms, to bring to this chapter.

In this chapter you will talk (1 + 0) and (0 + 1) phrases. You will also talk (1 + 1) VC and (1 + 1) CV phrases. You will have 94 different ways to express a 2 attack rhythm and ninety-three rhythm substitutes for, and variations on, any 2 attack rhythm.

As you anticipate talking these dabadaba rhythms, think about what you expect the difference between a (2 + 0) and a (0 + 2) rhythm to feel like. Similarly, what differences would you expect to notice with (2 + 1) CV and (1 + 2) VC phrases?

Reflect on the same questions after you have talked this chapter. Do your expectations line up, or not, with your actual dabadaba experience? Notice how your observations help you think about rhythm, in and out of tempo.

The advice to nail the rests in this chapter is always worth repeating. Pay close attention to accurately articulating rests, vowels and diphthongs--*in full*.

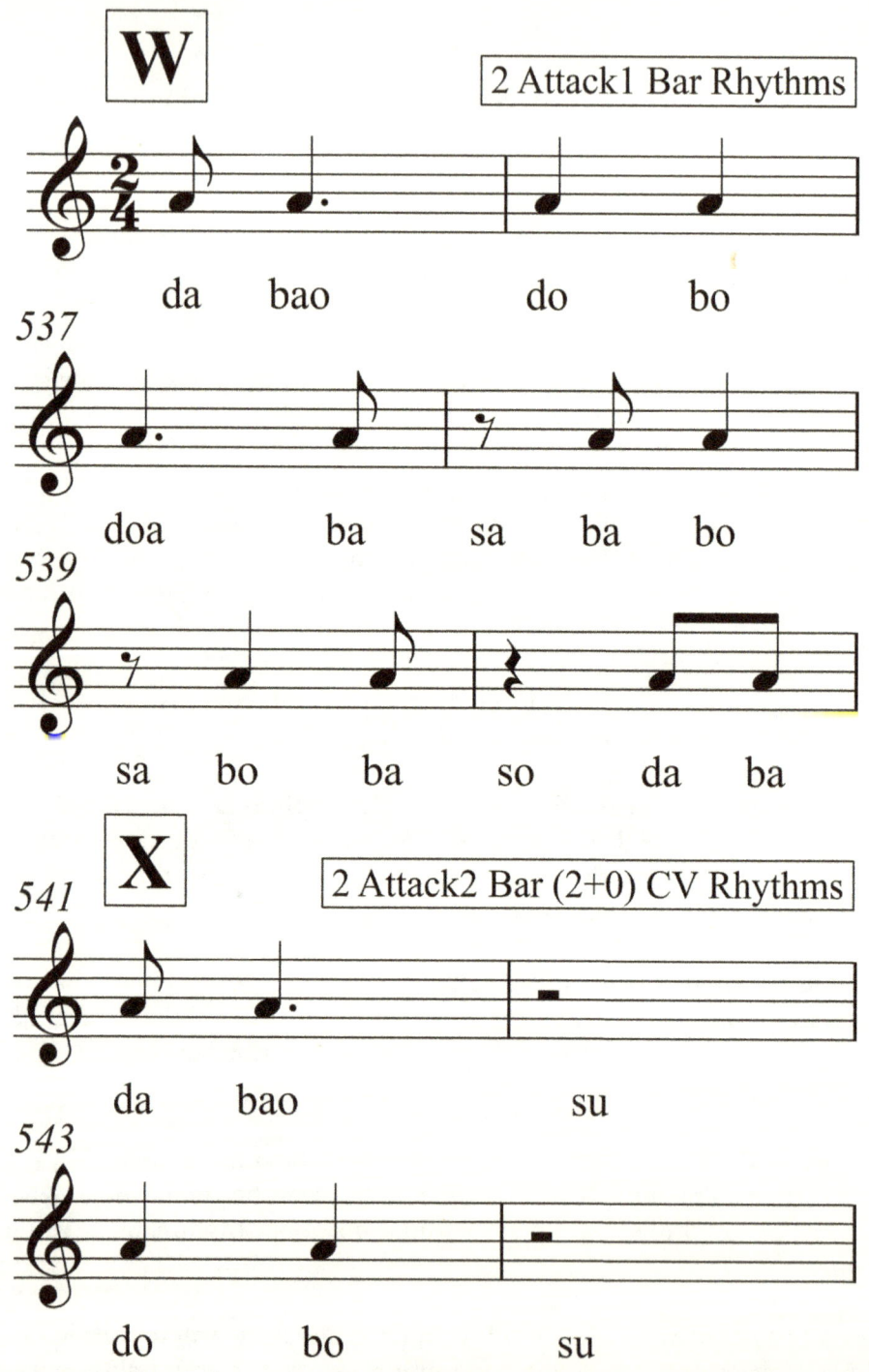

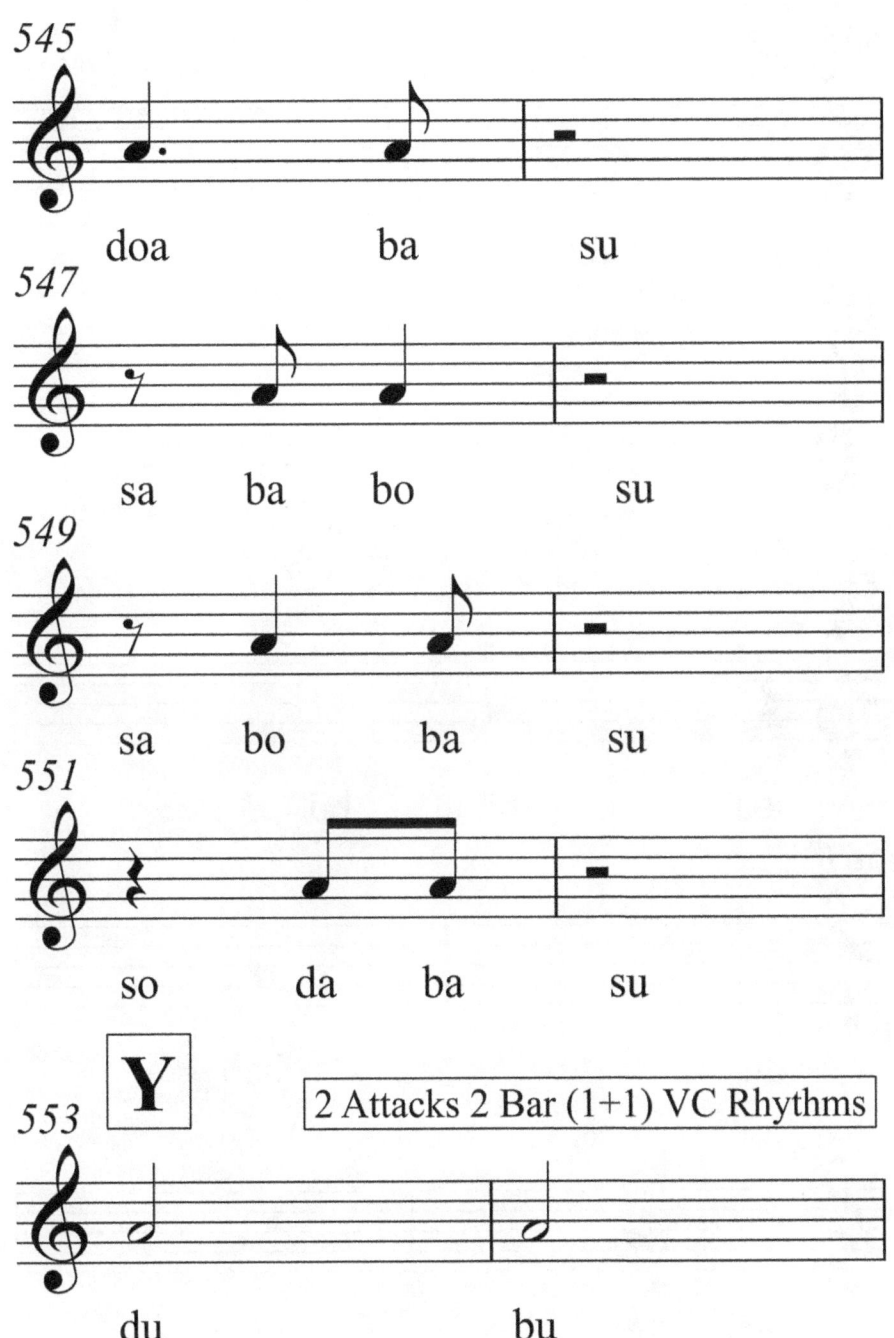

615

soa   ba   soa   ba

AA   2 Attack2 Bar (0+2) CV Rhythms

617

su   da   bao

619

su   do   bo

621

su   doa   ba

Chapter Eight: Talk 1 Attack Rhythms

In this chapter you talk, two bar, dabadaba rhythms, with a rhythm density of 1 attack.

When you talk one attack rhythms across two bars, you notice that three beats are not being attacked and the non-attacked beats are being occupied with a long vowel, diphthongs or rests.

With 1 attack rhythms you are, either, talking, an attacked long vowel, or diphthongs--for their *full* duration--or holding rested vowels or diphthongs--for their *full* duration.

With 1 attack dabadaba rhythms, articulating rests, tied vowels or diphthongs, are *critically* important to making these rhythms work.

Learning to feel comfortable with the space around 1 attack rhythms is one of the benefits students report to me after working with these rhythms. They also say they are much more aware of rhythm placement when they have only one note to work with.

In this chapter you will talk (1 + 0) and (0 + 1) dabadaba phrases. You will have eight different ways to express a 1 attack rhythm and seven rhythm substitutes for, and variations on, any 1 attack rhythm.

This might be useful to know when you need to come up with a variety of 1 attack rhythm hits for a song arrangement. This might be good to know, too, when you need to improvise a rhythm comment, in real time on your instrument, with only 1 attack.

As you prepare to talk these dabadaba rhythms, think about what you expect the difference between (1 + 0) and (0 + 1) phrases to feel like.

When you finish talking this chapter, reflect on these same questions: Did your expectations line up with your actual experience or not? Did this experience offer you fresh insights about rhythm, in and out of tempo?

Pay close attention to articulating rests and tied vowels--*in full*. Make the rests so defined and accurate that the single attack just pops right out!

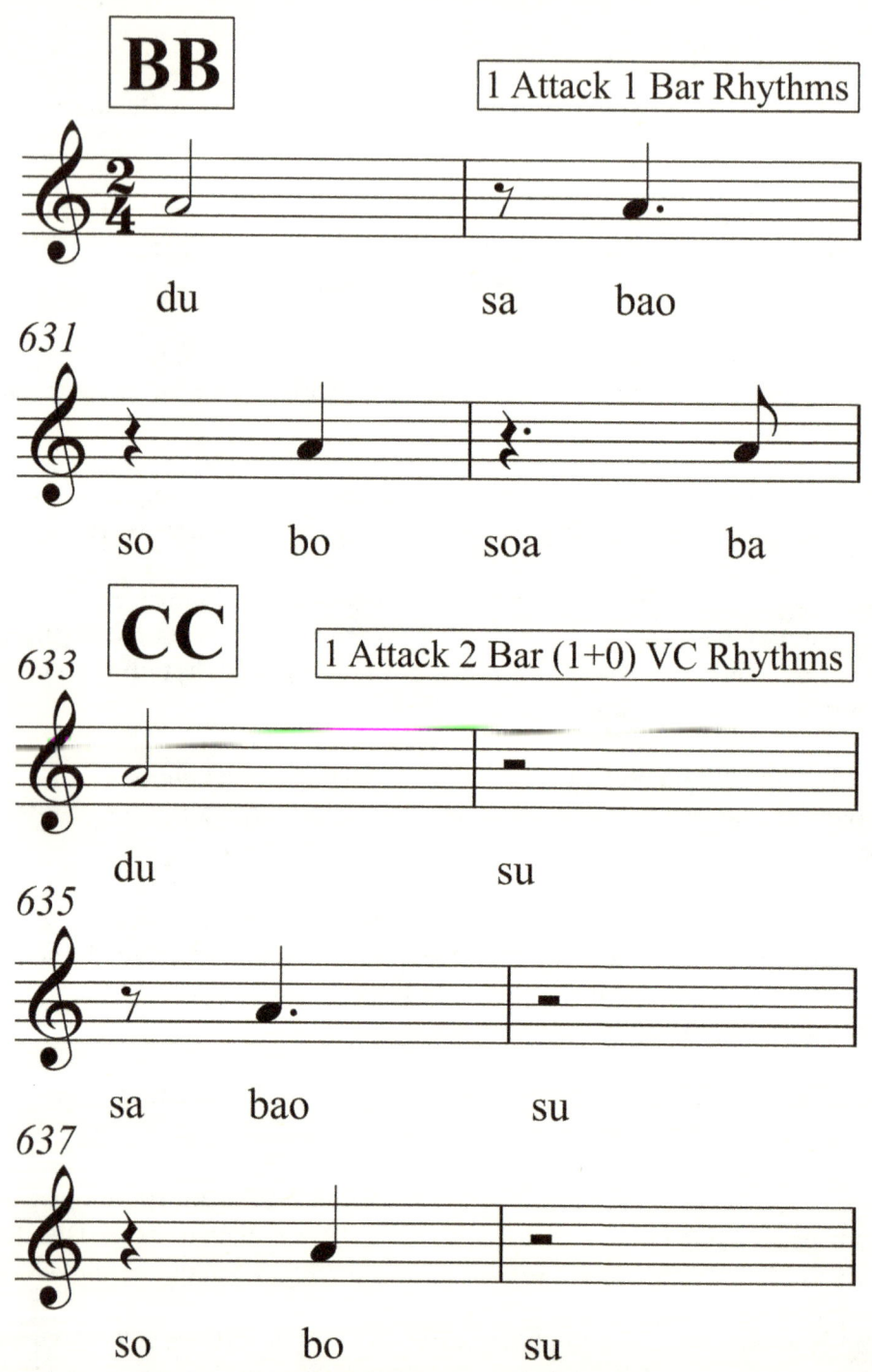

Chapter Nine: Talk Syncopated Rhythms

In this chapter you will talk only syncopated dabadaba rhythms. The five syncopated rhythms, native to the dabadaba vocabulary, isolated for you here, are bars 3, 6, 8, 10 and 13.

You have met all these syncopated dabadaba rhythms in previous chapters. The rhythms are not new to you. However, how they combine with each other, in this chapter, in two bar syncopated phrases, will be.

Although they are not explicitly organised by rhythmic density in this chapter, it is clear that there is one, 3 attack syncopated rhythm; three, 2 attack syncopated rhythms; and one, 1 attack syncopated rhythm

In section EE, there are five variable syncopated, eighth note, rhythms occurring in the strong bar while a su rest occupies the weak bar.

In section FF the variable syncopated rhythm occurs on the strong bar and the constant syncopated rhythm answers in the weak bar.

In section GG, the constant syncopated rhythm occurs on the strong bar and the variable syncopated rhythm answers in the weak bar.

You have these unmarked rhythm profiles available to you in this chapter: (3 + 0), (3 + 1), (3 + 2), (2 + 2), (2 + 2), (2 + 3), (1 + 3) and (0 + 3). You have fifty-five syncopated, dabadaba, phrases available to you in this chapter.

Defining syncopation is not as useful as talking syncopation at this stage. Rather than come up with some definition for syncopation, it's more useful for you to be able to say: "Here are the syncopated rhythms in the dabadaba vocabulary; daboba, dabao, doaba, saboba and sabao."

You can say, think and feel these syncopated rhythms, in tempo. You can't do that with a definition.

Chapter Ten: What You Have Learned

Congratulations! You have learned a lot through learning and talking dabadaba.

You learned a one bar dabadaba rhythm.

You learned a vocabulary of sixteen dabadaba eighth note rhythms, one word at time. You learned that fifteen of these rhythms derived from the one bar dabadaba rhythm.

You learned to talk the dabadaba vocabulary through 373 two bar phrases.

You talked each dabadaba rhythm several times in different contexts.

You talked dabadaba 32 times across the 758 bars.

You talked 3 attack rhythms one hundred and eighty-five times: namely, dababo 41 times, daboba 62 times, dodaba 41 times and sabadaba, 41 times.

You talked 2 attack rhythms three hundred and twenty-one times: specifically, dabao 65 times, dobo 44 times, doaba 64 times, sababo 38 times, saboba 66 times and sodaba, 44 times.

You talked 1 attack rhythms one hundred and eighty-five times: specifically, du 21 times, bu 20 times, sabao 62 times, sobo 41 times and soaba, 41 times. Finally you talked su 35 times.

The net result of all this activity is that you have had a thorough dabadaba experience. You spent 758 bars talking a sixteen bar dabadaba vocabulary in 373 different combinations.

You talked nine chapters of dabadaba rhythms, one **rhythm density** at a time. Within each chapter you talked different **rhythm profiles** and explored all the possibilities within one rhythm density level.

You talked one 8 attack rhythm, eight 7 attack rhythms, forty-four 6 attack rhythms, fifty-six 5 attack rhythms, one hundred 4 attack rhythms, fifty-eight 3 attack rhythms, forty-seven 2 attack rhythms, ten 1 attack rhythms and fifty-five syncopated rhythms.

You learned that each density level could be broken down to **attack profiles.** For example, 7 attack rhythms could be organised as 3 attack plus 4 attack rhythm profiles (3 + 4) and vice versa (4 + 3).

You learned how the principle of **rhythm alternation** (strong event alternating with weak event) and the concept of **rhythm density** can help you predict, and reflect, on the rhythm impact of any phrase.

In short, you have learned and talked the dabadaba's. You are now comfortable cutting and slicing dabadaba sixteen different ways, in 373 different contexts. That is no small achievement.

But there's more.

In talking these dabadaba rhythms you have trained your **ear** to hear them as rhythmisation words. You have trained your **eye** to see these, eighth note, rhythms as rhythmisation words and notation. You have trained your **speech** to say them, on demand, in any dabadaba context. These are important rhythm achievements that you can—rightfully--celebrate.

The next stage is to embed these dabadaba rhythms, as *physiological* instructions, in your body, *off* your instrument. The stage after that is to embed them as physiological instructions, in your body, *on* your instrument.

The objective of this book is to install these dabadaba rhythms in your mind and speech and to get you to talk all the rhythms once from bar 01 to 758. If you have done that, then that goal is achieved. Well done.

Now you can read this book again, and again, following along with the section, entitled How Long To Read This Book, on page XX in the appendices. Or, you can proceed directly to talking your way through Rhythm Book 103 Sixteenth Note Rhythm Patterns for All Musicians

Thank you for your interest and time. Thank you for reading this far. Thank you for making dabadaba part of your rhythm foundation.

How To Learn Dabadaba Words

Learn Sixteen Dabadaba Words in 8 Bar Sections

In this section you will introduce the sixteen word vocabulary to your mind, brain and speech system. You will teach yourself, step by step, to say and talk the following sixteen dabadaba words.

4 attack word: dabadaba.

3 attack words: dababo, daboba, dodaba, sabadaba.

2 attack words: dabao, dobo, doaba, sababo, saboba, sodaba.

1 attack words: du, sabao, sobo, soaba.

0 attack word: su.

So let's get started.

Step 01: Set your metronome to MM60. Pronounce the vowel a as in path. Say dabadaba 8 times like this. One click equals daba.

Dabadaba dabadaba dabadaba dabadaba
Dabadaba dabadaba dabadaba dabadaba

Then rest your mind for 8 clicks. Then take 8 clicks to prepare your mind and speech system to say the next rhythm in the next step.

Step 02: Say dobo 8 times as directed below. Pronounce the o vowel as in go. Each syllable is held for one full click. Ensure you hold do and bo for one full click each.

Dobo dobo dobo dobo
Dobo dobo dobo dobo

Then rest your mind for 8 clicks. Then take 8 clicks to prepare your mind and speech system to say the next rhythm in the next step.

Step 03: Say du bu 4 times as follows. Pronounce the u vowel as in blue. Each syllable is held for two full clicks. Ensure you hold du and bu for the full 2 clicks. Breathe like a singer or wind instrument player.

Du bu du bu
Du bu du bu

Then rest your mind for 8 clicks. Then take 8 clicks to prepare your mind and speech system to say the next rhythm in the next step.

Step 04: Say dababo 8 times as follows. Ensure you hold bo for the full one click.

Dababo dababo dababo dababo
Dababo dababo dababo dababo

Then rest your mind for 8 clicks. Then take 8 clicks to prepare your mind and speech system to say the next rhythm in the next step.

Step 05: Say daboba 8 times as follows.

Daboba daboba daboba daboba
Daboba daboba daboba daboba

Then rest your mind for 8 clicks. Then take 8 clicks to prepare your mind and speech system to say the next rhythm in the next step.

Step 06: Say dodaba 8 times as follows. Ensure you hold do for the full click.

Dodaba dodaba dodaba dodaba
Dodaba dodaba dodaba dodaba

Then rest your mind for 8 clicks. Then take 8 clicks to prepare your mind and speech system to say the next rhythm in the next step.

Step 07: Say sabadaba 8 times as follows. One click equals saba or daba.

Sabadaba sabadaba sabadaba sabadaba
Sabadaba sabadaba sabadaba sabadaba

Then rest your mind for 8 clicks. Then take 8 clicks to prepare your mind and speech system to say the next rhythm in the next step.

Step 08: Say dabao 8 times as follows. Ensure you hold bao for the full duration.

Dabao dabao dabao dabao
Dabao dabao dabao dabao

Then rest your mind for 8 clicks. Then take 8 clicks to prepare your mind and speech system to say the next rhythm in the next step.

Step 09: Say doaba 8 times as follows. Ensure you hold doa for the full duration.

Doaba doaba doaba doaba
Doaba doaba doaba doaba

Then rest your mind for 8 clicks. Then take 8 clicks to prepare your mind and speech system to say the next rhythm in the next step.

Step 10: Say sababo 8 times as follows. Ensure you hold bo for the full one click duration.

Sababo sababo sababo sababo
Sababo sababo sababo sababo

Then rest your mind for 8 clicks. Then take 8 clicks to prepare your mind and speech system to say the next rhythm in the next step.

Step 11: Say saboba 8 times as follows. Ensure you hold bo for the full duration. Beware of the upbeat attacks of bo and ba.

Saboba saboba saboba saboba
Saboba saboba saboba saboba

Then rest your mind for 8 clicks. Then take 8 clicks to prepare your mind and speech system to say the next rhythm in the next step.

Step 12: Say sodaba 8 times as follows. Ensure you hold so for the full one click duration.

Sodaba sodaba sodaba sodaba
Sodaba sodaba sodaba sodaba

Then rest your mind for 8 clicks. Then take 8 clicks to prepare your mind and speech system to say the next rhythm in the next step.

Step 13: Say sabao 8 times as follows. Ensure you hold bao for the full diphthong duration.

Sabao sabao sabao sabao
Sabao sabao sabao sabao

Then rest your mind for 8 clicks. Then take 8 clicks to prepare your mind and speech system to say the next rhythm in the next step.

Step 14: Say sobo 8 times as follows. Ensure you hold so and bo for the full one click duration.

Sobo sobo sobo sobo
Sobo sobo sobo sobo

Then rest your mind for 8 clicks. Then take 8 clicks to prepare your mind and speech system to say the next rhythm in the next step.

Step 15: Say soaba 8 times as follows. Ensure you hold soa for the full diphthong duration.

Soaba soaba soaba soaba
Soaba soaba soaba soaba

Then rest your mind for 8 clicks. Then take 8 clicks to prepare your mind and speech system to say the next rhythm in the next step.

Step 16: Say su 8 times as follows. Ensure you hold su for the full two clicks.

Su su su su
Su su su su

Turn off the metronome. Relax.

Step 17: Take a 2 minute rest. Let your mind wander. Let your subconscious librarians archive all the learning you have just done for convenient retrieval in the future. Let your mind save everything to disc. Acknowledge that your mind has just done concentrated work and that it has now earned a, well deserved, rest.

Learn Sixteen Dabadaba Sounds with Notation Instructions

In the following nine pages, you can simply set your metronome to MM60 and read and talk along with the notation and rhythmisation.

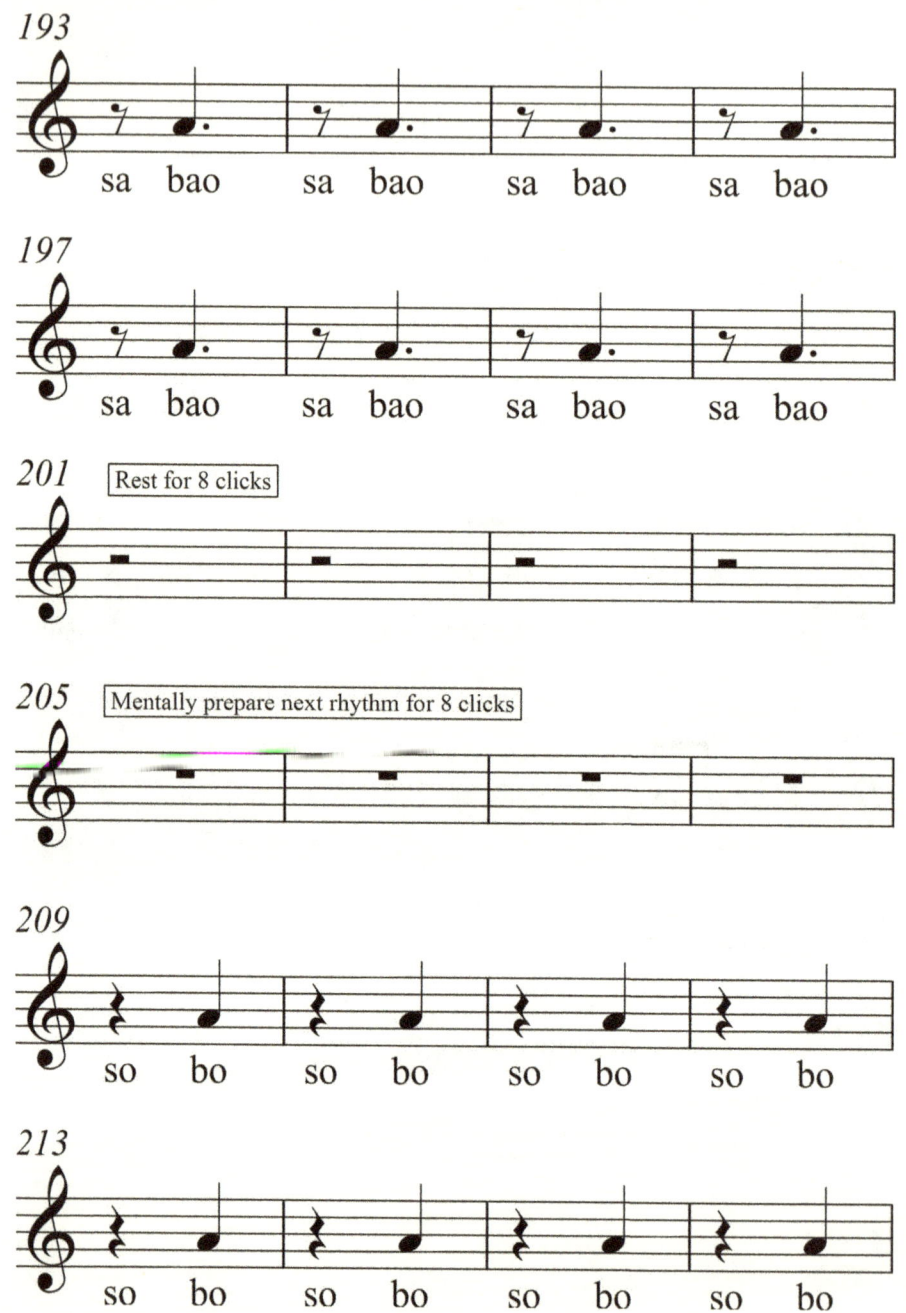

Now that you have learned this vocabulary, you can start talking and reading the rhythm phrases section. Or, if you need more work learning the dabadaba words before proceeding, you can do one, or all, of the following three processes.

Learn Sixteen Dabadaba Words in 12 Bar Sections

Repeat the previous exercise with 12 repetitions instead of 8. The objectives are twofold. One, is to give you practice at isolating and saying each rhythm. Two, to give you experience saying the rhythm within the 12 bar blues form.

You will feel a 12 bar form as you say the rhythm 12 times. You will feel the form as well as the surface rhythm. While, technically, you are feeling bars of 2/4, the bigger benefit is that you are *feeling rhythm in 2*--rather than feeling rhythm in 4--as you would with 4/4 or dobodobo, as in Rhythm Book 01. Being able to feel a form makes getting lost---when you are jamming or improvising--so much harder.

Learn Sixteen Dabadaba Words in 16 Bar Sections

Repeat the previous exercise with 16 repetitions instead of 12. The objectives are the same. One objective is to give you practise at isolating and saying each rhythm. The second objective is to give you experience saying the rhythm within a 16 bar form.

Sixteen bars is, typically, the length of two verses or a bridge and last verse in typical standard jazz and pop tunes. Again you are feeling form as well as surface rhythm. The technical--rhythm--benefit mentioned above, applies here too. Very cool.

Learn Sixteen Dabadaba Words in 32 Bar Sections

Repeat the previous exercise with 32 repetitions instead of 16. The twofold objectives remain the same. The first aim is to give you practise at isolating and saying each rhythm. The second goal is to give you experience saying the rhythm within a thirty-two bar form.

Thirty-two bars is the, typical, length of a standard jazz and pop tune. Be aware that you are feeling form as well as surface rhythm when you repeat any dabadaba rhythm 32 times. The technical--rhythm--benefit mentioned above, applies here too.

Frequently Asked Questions

Why does saying the d and b in the prescribed place matter?

Whenever you say do, du, duo or de you are saying an event that starts on the strong beat, the strong half of the bar or on the strong bar. Whenever you say bo, bu, bou or be you are saying an event that starts on the weak beat, the weak half of the bar or on the weak bar.

By specifying whether any rhythm is a weak or strong event (the same rhythm can be weak or strong) you are mindful of the principle of rhythmic alternation operating. Knowing whether events are weak or strong enables you to feel surface and underlying rhythm *simultaneously*.

In short, the specific consonants are signposts that prevent you from getting lost in any music you are playing. And when you do get lost, they help you find your place again quicker.

How does saying the d and b in the prescribed place help a rhythm guitar player?

Any d led syllable means you down pick or down strum that syllable. Any b led syllable means you up pick or up strum that syllable. In other words, the consonants are specific picking and strumming instructions.

How is each rhythm derived from dabadaba?

Each surface dabadaba rhythm is related to the underlying dabadaba rhythm by between one to six steps.

I'll simply list each rhythm and their derivations from dabadaba to surface rhythm.

I'll walk you through the steps for two of the sixteen rhythms.

Example 01: dabadaba > daba_aba > dabaaba > daboba

For the daboba rhythm, start with dabadaba, remove the third consonant to read daba_aba, combine a_a into aa then rewrite aa as an o vowel to now read daboba.

Example 02: dabadaba > da_ada_a > daadaa > dodo > dobo

For the dobo rhythm, start with dabadaba, remove the second and fourth consonants to now read da_ada_a, rewrite a_a as aa then rewrite aa as an o vowel to now read dodo, then comply with the principle of alternation and rewrite as dobo

Here are the remaining dabadaba rhythms with their derivations from dabadaba.

3 attack rhythms

dabadaba > dabada_a > dabadaa > dabado > dababo >

dabadaba> daba_aba > dabaaba > daboba

dabadaba > da_adaba > daadaba > dodaba

dabadaba > sabadaba

2 attack rhythms

dabadaba > daba_a_a > daba_aa > daba_o > dabao

dabadaba > da_ada_a > daadaa > dodo > dobo

dabadaba > da_a_aba > daa_aba > do_aba > doaba

dabadaba > dabada_a > dabadaa > dabado > dababo > sababo

dabadaba > daba_aba > dabaaba > daboba > saboba

dabadaba > da_adaba > daadaba > dodaba > sodaba

XVIII

1 attack rhythms

dabadaba > da_a_ a _a > daa_aa > do_o > doo > du

dabadaba > daba_a_a > daba_aa > daba_o > dabao > sabao

dabadaba > da_ada_a > daadaa > dodo > dobo > sobo

dabadaba > da_a_aba > daa_aba > do_aba > doaba > soaba >

These derivations give you a detailed understanding of how each rhythm derives from dabadaba, how they all belong to the dabadaba vocabulary and in what *specific* sense they can each be called a dabadaba rhythm.

Do I keep the tempo in my hands or feet?

Keep the tempo in your feet. Keep the melodic rhythm in your speech and/or hands. In this book you are talking melodic rhythm.

What tempo rhythm should I use?

In the beginning, many rhythmisation students default to a dabadaba tempo rhythm so that their feet and speech are using the same rhythm level. Your rhythm will sound stiff and wooden, when you do this.

If you want a flowing rhythm effect, then, play dobodobo in your feet while you talk dabadaba. This is the first tempo rhythm you should learn and practise. Firstly, with a metronome set to a dobodobo tempo, play dobodobo rhythm tempo in your feet, while you talk dabadaba. Secondly, repeat the same process without a metronome.

If you want an even more relaxed, confident, rhythm effect, then play dubudubu in your feet while you talk dabadaba. Firstly, with a metronome set to a dobodobo tempo, play dubudubu rhythm tempo in your feet, while you talk dabadaba. Secondly, repeat the same process without a metronome.

By training your feet to play dobodobo or dubudubu, while talking dabadaba, you are teaching yourself to master tempo rhythm and melodic rhythm *simultaneously*. The place for dabadaba is in the melodic rhythm. The place for dobodobo is in the metronome click and in the feet.

How long to read the whole book?

At a continuous tempo of MM60 it would take you 26 minutes to read every single bar the first time.

This book contains 1,516 beats of notation and rhythmisation. Your first task is to read through the book once. Then, periodically read, talk and play all the chapters, one to ten, one session at a time.

This table below outlines how long (to the nearest minute) each session will take you at any given tempo. Take your time. Enjoy.

Example:
At a continuous tempo of MM84 it would take you 18 minutes to read every single bar.

Tempo	Minutes
MM 60	26
MM 64	24
MM 68	23
MM 72	21
MM 76	20
MM 80	19
MM 84	18
MM 88	17
MM 92	17
MM 96	16
MM 100	15
MM 104	15
MM 108	14
MM 112	14
MM 116	13
MM 120	13
MM 124	12

Do you count rhythm with rhythmisation?

Counting rhythm is one rhythm learning and measuring system and rhythmisation is another. You can use both systems. The author uses rhythm counting for *out* of tempo analysis and measurement of *static rhythm* and he uses rhythmisation for *in* tempo *dynamic* rhythm description. The author uses rhythmisation over ninety-five percent of the time, and counting, the other five percent of the time.

Rhythm counting describes only the attack and not the duration of any rhythm. Rhythmisation describes both. Saying any rhythm word with the correct vowel duration *automatically* gives you the correct rhythm.

Is Rhythmisation the only rhythm verbalisation system?

No. There are several others: some new, some centuries old. The Carnatic vocal system of Konnokol or Solkattu is an old rhythm verbalisation system. In her 1998 Masters in Music Performance thesis entitled "KONNAKOL The History and Development of Solkattu - the Vocal Syllables - of the Mridangam", Lisa Young gives you a well documented introduction. For more information, visit www.lisayoung.com.au

Another verbalisation system gaining traction in the west is Takadimi. The Takadimi system of rhythm pedagogy is described in "Takadimi: A Beat-Oriented System of Rhythm Pedagogy," Journal of Music Theory Pedagogy, 1996, by Hoffman, Pelto, and White. For more information, visit www.takadimi.net.

Rhythmisation was first taught in Auckland, New Zealand, in 1982, some 14 years before the cited Konnokol and Takadimi works were published and 17 years before the author gained, dial up, internet access in 1999.

Some African rhythm verbalisation traditions are described in African Rhythm and African Sensibility, by John Miller Chernoff.

There are other rhythmisation systems used in primary and secondary schools including Kodaly, Orff and Edward E. Gordon, amongst others.

How does knowing dobodobo help the jazz, rock and pop musician?

The first thing you need to be able to do, in western commercial music, is keep the beat. Being able to keep the beat through any dobodobo rhythm is the most basic music skill required.

Rockers, jazzers and pop musicians deal mostly in dabadaba, eighth note, melodic rhythms. These rhythms are divisions of what? They are divisions of the dobodobo or quarter note rhythm. When you know your dobodobo's you can divide them into dabadaba's. When you don't know them you can't.

How does knowing dobodobo help the blues and reggae musician?

Blues and reggae styles are largely characterised by dibidibi melodic rhythms. Dibidibi rhythms are divisions of the dabadaba rhythms and subdivisions of the dobodobo rhythms. When you know your dobodobo's you can divide them into dabadaba eighth notes, and further subdivide them into dibidibi sixteenth notes.

The most convincing dibidibi performances are those supported by a strong dabadaba framework which is, in turn, supported by a strong dobodobo framework.

The wimpiest sixteenth note rhythm performances are those that are not supported by strong dabadaba and dobodobo frameworks.

How does dobodobo help with odd subdivisions?

Dobodobo provides you with the framework you need to be able to subdivide any quarter note into any triplet, quintuplet and septuplet value.

What is the principle of rhythmic alternation?

Alternation in music reflects alternations that occur in the natural world: alternating tides coming in and out, sun rising and setting, moon rising and setting, up and down, happy and sad and so on.

The key rhythmic alternation in music is strong versus weak.

Strong bars (odd numbered bars) versus weak bars (even numbered bars). Strong beats (odd numbered beats) versus weak beats (even numbered beats). Strong beat divisions versus weak beat divisions. Strong beat subdivisions versus weak beat subdivisions.

Rhythmic alternations are also denoted by terms like, off and on the beat, the downbeat and the upbeat.

Understanding the principle of rhythmic alternation greatly benefits you in many ways, including expanding your rhythmic awareness, deepening your rhythmic sensitivity and better equipping you to write and play strong melody.

The hierarchy of strong-weak rhythm alternation is displayed here.

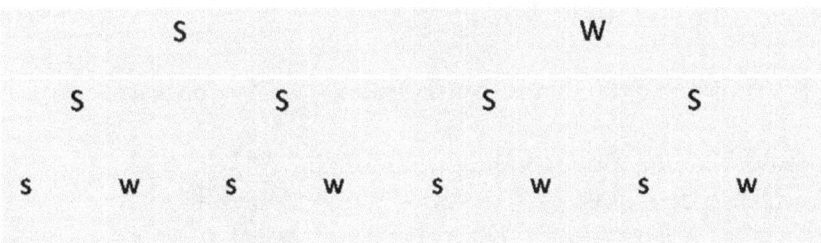

For the purposes of dabadaba you can think of the three S W levels from top to bottom as representing du bu, dividing into do bo do bo, dividing into da ba da ba da ba da ba, as illustrated below.

		du				bu	
do		bo		do		bo	
da	ba	da	ba	da	ba	da	ba

What's an example of a dabadaba song?

Bessie's Blues by John Coltrane is an example of a dabadaba song. Here the melodic rhythm is rhythmised as one bar phrases.

Bar lines are indicated by a barline | symbol or a tilde ~ symbol.

dodabau | dodabuba | dababodaboba~abadabau |
sabobadabaso | doabasaboba | dababodaboba~abadabasaboba |
dobododaba | dababodabao | sabadabasu | sudabadaba |

Vowels separated by the tilde ~ symbol indicate tied notes across a bar line. Example: ba~a is rhythmisation for an eighth note tied across a bar line to the first eighth note in the next bar. The tilde sign ~ tells you that durations either side of ~ are tied.

Here is the melodic rhythm is rhythmised as two bar phrases.

dodabau dodabuba | dababodabobobadabau
sabobadabaso doabasaboba | dababodabobobadabasaboba
dobododaba dababodabao | sabadabasu sudabadaba

In this example, two single bars tied by a ~ sign, dababodaboba~abadabau, are rewritten as dababodabobobadabau where ba~a is rewritten as *bo*.

Similarly dababodaboba~abadabasaboba is rewritten as dababodabobobadabasaboba

Rhythmisation Glossary

Term	Definition
1e+a	The name of a rhythm counting system.
Attack	Where the duration of a rhythm starts. In rhythmisation an attack is indicated by a consonant.
Attacks	The number of sounded consonants in a rhythm word.
Attack Profile	A synonym for rhythm profile
Call and Response	A rhythm phrase where one rhythm calls and another rhythm answers in response. The phrase could be of any length, usually four bars or less.
Click	A metronome click.
Calling Rhythm	The first rhythm in a call and response rhythm phrase. The calling rhythm occurs on the strong part of the phrase.
Counting Rhythm	A system for identifying rhythm attack patterns but not durations.
Dababa Dababa	The name of the triple eighth note rhythmisation vocabulary in 6/8.
Dabadaba	The name of the eighth note rhythmisation vocabulary in 2/4.
Dabadaba	The eighth note rhythm level.
Dabadaba Dabadaba	The name of the eighth note rhythmisation vocabulary in 4/4.
Dabadabadaba	The name of the eighth note rhythmisation vocabulary in 3/4.
Debedebe	The name of the whole note rhythmisation vocabulary in 4/4.
Debedebe	The whole note rhythm level.

Derived Rhythm	Any rhythm that belongs to a vocabulary and derives from the same seed or parent rhythm as other rhythms in the same vocabulary.
DibibiDibibi	The name of the triple sixteenth note rhythmisation vocabulary in 1/4.
Dibidibi	The name of the sixteenth note rhythmisation vocabulary in 1/4.
Dibidibi	The sixteenth note rhythm level.
Dibidibi Dibidibi	The name of the sixteenth note rhythmisation vocabulary in 2/4.
Diphthong	A co-occurrence of two or more vowels.
Diphthong Rhythm	A duration containing two or more different vowels indicating equivalence to dotted or tied notation rhythms or syncopated rhythms.
Dobobo	The name of the triplet quarter note rhythmisation vocabulary in 3/4.
Dobodobo	The name of the quarter note rhythmisation vocabulary in 4/4.
Dobodobo	The quarter note rhythm level.
Dububu	The name of the triplet half note rhythmisation vocabulary in 3/2.
Dubudubu	The name of the half note rhythmisation vocabulary in 4/4.
Dubudubu	The half note rhythm level.
Dynamic Rhythm	Rhythm in tempo.
Harmonic Rhythm	The rhythm level or vocabulary used by the harmony or chord changes in a song. Debe, dubu and duobo are the most common harmonic rhythms.

Main rhythm	Refers to the most frequent rhythm vocabulary used in a piece of music.
Melodic Rhythm	The rhythm (level or vocabulary) used by the melody.
Parent rhythm	A synonym for seed rhythm.
Pataka	The triplet eighth note rhythm level.
Pataka Pataka	The name of the triplet eighth note rhythmisation vocabulary in 2/4.
Pataka Pataka Pataka Pataka	The name of the triplet eighth note rhythmisation vocabulary in 4/4.
Pitiki	The triplet sixteenth note rhythm level.
Pitiki Pitiki	The name of the triplet sixteenth note rhythmisation vocabulary in 1/4
Pitiki Pitiki Pitiki Pitiki	The name of the triplet sixteenth note rhythmisation vocabulary in 2/4.
Potoko	The triplet quarter note rhythm level.
Potoko Potoko	The triplet quarter note rhythm vocabulary.
Putuku	The triplet half note rhythm level.
Putuku Putuku	The triplet half note rhythm vocabulary.
Response Rhythm	The rhythm that answers a calling rhythm in a call and response phrase.
Rhythm Balance	Refers to the balance between phrases within a rhythm profile. For example which balance do you want for a 7A, 2 bar rhythm phrase? 7+0, 6+1, 5+2, 4+3, 3+4, 2+5, 1+6 or 0+7? Which bar do you want to have the most rhythm attacks in? The strong or weak bar?
Rhythm Density	Refers to the number of attacks — sounded consonants — in a rhythm or rhythm phrase. A 7A attack rhythm means there are 7 attacks — sounded

Rhythm Profile	consonants—in the phrase. Rhythm Density gives you an idea of how active a given rhythm phrase is. A more detailed description of rhythm density. For example, 2 bar 7 attack rhythms can be broken into the following rhythm profiles: 7+0, 6+1, 5+2, 4+3, 3+4, 2+5, 1+6, 0+7.
Rhythm Level	Refers to the *level* of the whole note, half note, quarter note, eighth note or sixteenth note or triplet whole note, triplet half note, triplet quarter note, triplet eighth note or triplet sixteenth note. Any one of these values is a rhythm level.
Rhythm Phrase	A sequence of rhythm words.
Rhythm Position	The position of any rhythm event in the bar or phrase. Rhythm counting counts four quarter notes as 1 2 3 4. Each numeral denotes the ordinal position of each quarter note. Dobodobo describes the same rhythm. The consonants d and b, respectively, denote the strong and weak position of each quarter note in the phrase. You can use both approaches interchangeably.
Rhythm Resolution	A smallest rhythm level used in a composition. For example, a song may be mostly dobodobo but there are, say, three bars with dibidibi notes included. The rhythm resolution for this song is dibidibi.
Rhythm Substitution	Any act of substituting one rhythm for another. You may substitute any rhythm with a rhythm from the same or different profile in the same or different rhythm density, according

	to the degree of similarity or difference you are after.
Rhythm Variation	Similar to rhythm substitution.
Rhythm Vocabulary	Any group of rhythms derived from a seed rhythm or a parent rhythm. Any rhythm can be both a seed rhythm for one vocabulary and a derived rhythm in other vocabularies
Rhythm Weighting	Synonym for rhythm balance.
Rhythm Word	A sequence of rhythmisation syllables.
Rhythmic Alternation	The underlying rhythm alternation between strong and weak events on any rhythm level.
Rhythmification	The process of rhythmisation.
Rhythmifier	Somebody who rhythmises.
Rhythmify	A synonym for rhythmise.
Rhythmisation	Rhythmisation is the term coined by Taura Eruera to denote a system for verbalising rhythm with syllables and writing rhythm in simple English text, rather than music notation.
Rhythmisation Consonant b	The b consonant precedes any sounded vowel or diphthong that occurs on a weak duple rhythm position, division or subdivision.
Rhythmisation Consonant d	The d consonant precedes any sounded vowel or diphthong that occurs on a strong duple rhythm position, division or subdivision.
Rhythmisation Consonant k	The k consonant precedes any sounded vowel or diphthong that occurs on the third triplet rhythm position, division or subdivision.

Rhythmisation Consonant p	The p consonant precedes any sounded vowel or diphthong that occurs on the first triplet rhythm position, division or subdivision.
Rhythmisation Consonant s	The s consonant precedes any silent or unsounded vowel or diphthong that occurs on any duple rhythm position, division or subdivision, strong or weak.
Rhythmisation Consonant t	The t consonant precedes any sounded vowel or diphthong that occurs on the second triplet rhythm position, division or subdivision.
Rhythmisation Consonant z	The z consonant precedes any silent or unsounded vowel or diphthong that occurs on any triplet position, division or subdivision, strong or weak.
Rhythmisation Consonants	The main rhythmisation consonants are d, b, s, p, t, k, z.
Rhythmisation Text	When rhythm is written out in plain English text rather than notation.
Rhythmisation Vowel a	a (as in path) to indicate eighth note duration.
Rhythmisation Vowel e	e (as in bed) to indicate whole note duration.
Rhythmisation Vowel i	i (as in beat) to indicate sixteenth note duration.
Rhythmisation Vowel o	o (as in go) to indicate quarter note duration.
Rhythmisation Vowel u	u (as in blue) to indicate half note duration.
Rhythmisation Vowels	The five main rhythmisation vowels are: a, e, i, o, u.

Rhythmisations	A sequence of rhythmisation syllables, words and phrases
Secondary rhythm	Refers to the second most frequent rhythm vocabulary in a piece, which generally, occupies less than 20% of the piece.
Seed rhythm	Any single rhythm that a vocabulary is derived from.
Solmisation	Solmisation represents pitch with syllables rather than notation. India has used solmisation systems since 1300-1000 BC while Guido D'Arezzo created the solmisation do-re-mi system in the 10th century.
Static Rhythm	Rhythm that is written down or analysed out of tempo.
Syncopation	Indicated by diphthongs or co-occurring different vowels.
Syncopation Density	The number of consecutive syncopated events in a phrase.
Tempo Rhythm	The rhythm level that is kept in the foot and is usually twice as long as the melodic rhythm level.
Tertiary rhythm	Refers to the third most frequent rhythm vocabulary in a piece, which generally, occupies less than 5% of the piece.
Tilde	This symbol ~ occurs between two vowels in a diphthong to indicate where a bar line occurs in a duration.

XXXII

About the Author

I am Taura Eruera and I live in Grey Lynn, Auckland, New Zealand. Apart from a decade off in the 90's I have taught guitar continuously since 1982. That experience included teaching harmony, rhythm and guitar at the School of Creative Musicianship for six years followed by private teaching, seminars and clinics.

Over the years I have written many titles for guitar, melody, harmony and rhythm instruction. My titles have been self published for in-house and private student consumption or for publication on self owned websites. Over this time my energy has been focused more on creation than distribution. Now with platforms like Amazon Kindle available, I am formatting my catalogue of work for wider distribution.

Much of my writing has come out of my studies with Dick Grove, Howard Roberts and, more importantly, directly out of my teaching experience. I am grateful to a crazy diamond of a guitar player named Clash for being my pioneer rhythmisation dabadaba student, way back in the day. Clash reckoned that his skill in verbalising the Dabadaba's enabled him to put his strumming and picking hand on auto pilot, which made life that much easier for him at the Guitar Institute of Technology.

Guitar teaching has been a major activity for me over the years. Teaching has always alternated with gigging and other activities in my work life: old school, session work before the computer; transcription and lead sheet preparation and digital session work after computers came in. These activities extended to business consultation, business startups, founding roles in radio and health care companies, software development and search engine optimization services.

Even though I am involved in many interests, guitar teaching remains an important part of my week. Writing up those insights remains an important part of my teaching.

Join Rhythmisation Insights

Thank you for reading this book. I hope you find this book useful and thorough. Let me invite you to join the Rhythmisation Insights Group.

Simply paste this URL into your web browser -- https://tinyurl.com/dabadabavol01

You will be redirected to a page where you can enter your details in the sign up form and join the discoveries!

Expect lots of useful information that we just couldn't include in this book. Expect real life resources from real people like you sharing their experiences and insights with you. See you on the inside.

Kind regards,
Taura

www.ingramcontent.com/pod-product-compliance
Lightning Source LLC
Chambersburg PA
CBHW051652040426
42446CB00009B/1102